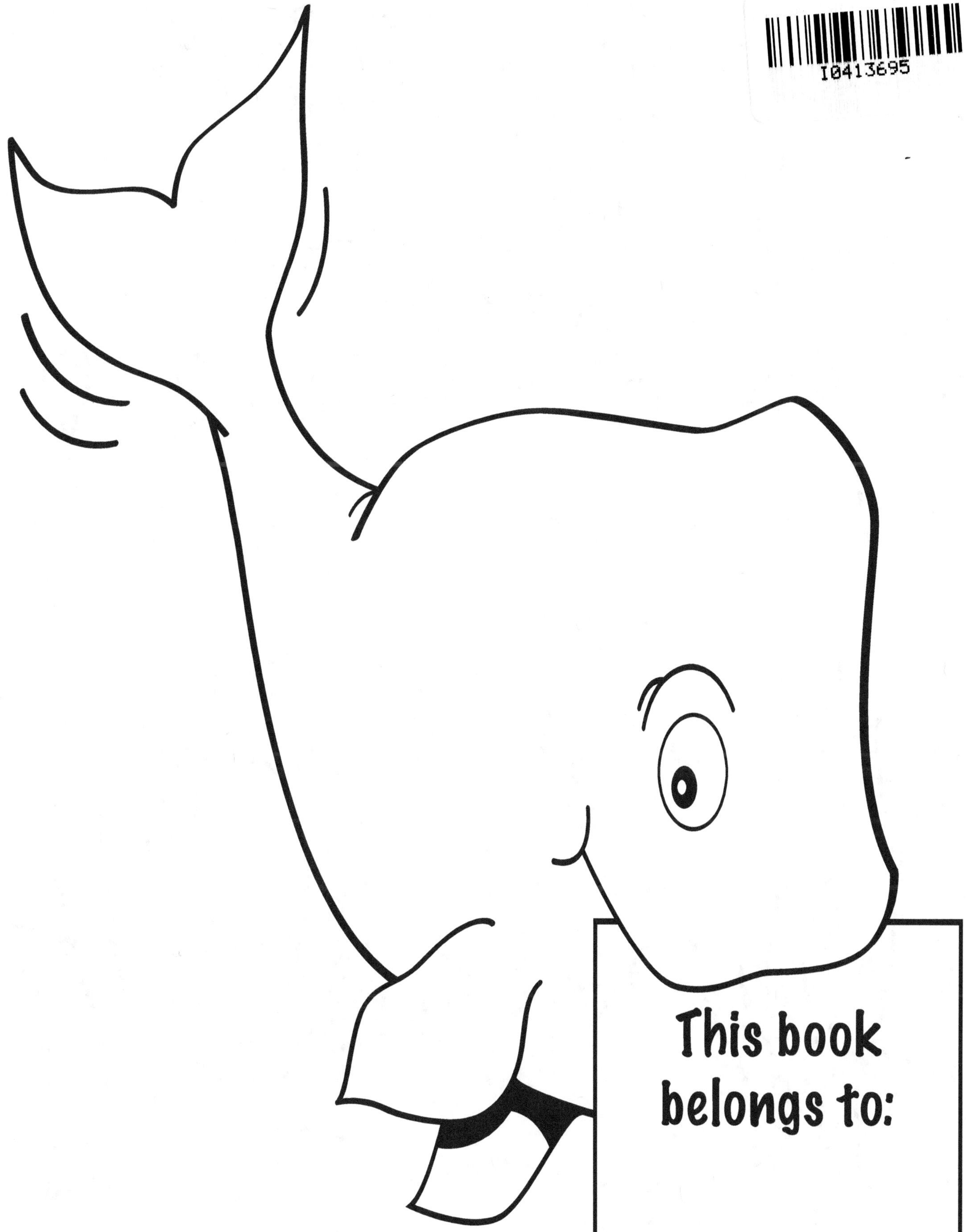
This book
belongs to:

Finding Fish & Marine Life

Coloring Book

Mary Lou Brown & Sandy Mahony

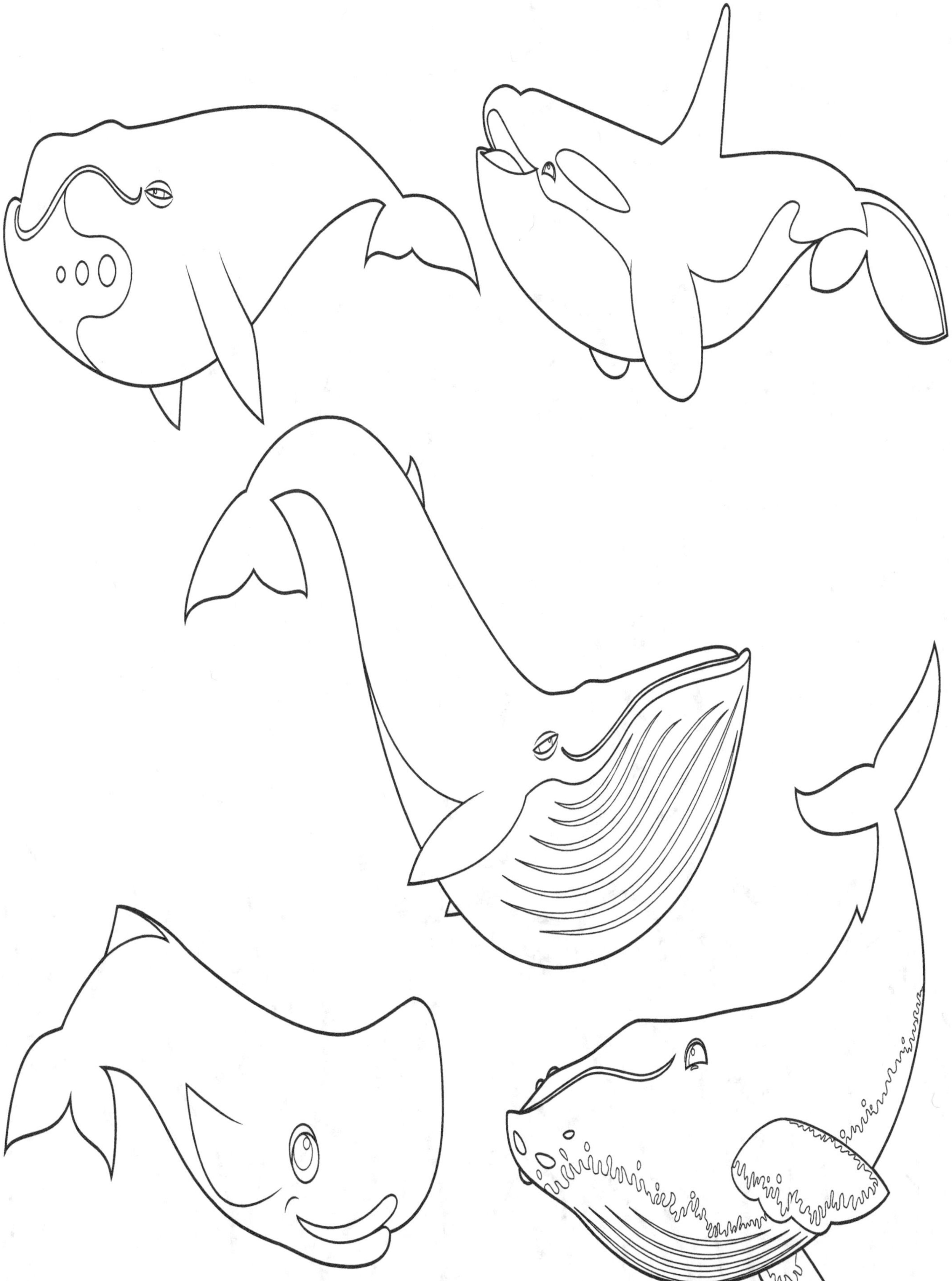

Adventure
Learning Press

www.ingramcontent.com/pod-product-compliance
Lightning Source LLC
Chambersburg PA
CBHW081123280526
45787CB00007B/2959
9781535006941